Tales—
Clever, Foolish, and Brave

Ron Benson

Lynn Bryan

Kim Newlove

Charolette Player

Liz Stenson

CONSULTANTS

Susan Elliott

Diane Lomond

Ken MacInnis

Elizabeth Parchment

Annetta Probst

Prentice Hall Ginn Canada
Scarborough, Ontario

Contents

Bibliography

🎧 Selections with this symbol are available on audio.

  This symbol indicates student writing.

🍁 Canadian selections are marked with this symbol.

From Tiger to Anansi

by Philip Sherlock
Illustrated by Sylvie Bourbonnière

Once upon a time and a long long time ago the Tiger was king of the forest.

At evening when all the animals sat together in a circle and talked and laughed together, Snake would ask:

"Who is the strongest of us all?"

"Tiger is strongest," cried Dog. "When Tiger whispers the trees listen. When Tiger is angry and cries out, the trees tremble."

"And who is the weakest of all?" asked Snake.

"Anansi," shouted Dog, and they all laughed together. "Anansi the spider is weakest of all. When he whispers no one listens. When he shouts everyone laughs."

Now one day the weakest and the strongest came face to face, Ansansi and Tiger. They met in a clearing of the forest. The frogs hiding under the cool leaves saw them. The bright green parrots in the branches heard them.

When they met, Anansi bowed so low that his forehead touched the ground. Tiger did not greet him. Tiger just looked at Anansi.

"Good morning, Tiger," cried Anansi. "I have a favor to ask."

"And what is it, Anansi?" said Tiger.

"Tiger, we all know that you are strongest of us all. This is why we give your name to many things. We have Tiger lilies and Tiger stories and Tiger moths, and Tiger this and Tiger that. Everyone knows that I am weakest of all. This is why nothing bears my name. Tiger, let something be called after the weakest one so that people may know my name too."

"Well," said Tiger, without so much as a glance toward Anansi, "what would you like to bear your name?"

"The stories," cried Anansi. "The stories that we tell in the forest at evening time when the sun goes down, the stories about Br'er Snake and Br'er Tacumah, Br'er Cow and Br'er Bird and all of us."

Now Tiger liked these sories and he meant to keep them as Tiger stories. He thought to himself, How stupid, how weak this Anansi is. I will play a trick on him so that all the animals will laugh at him. Tiger moved his tail slowly from side to side and said, "Very good, Anansi, very good. I will let the stories be named after you, if you do what I ask."

"Tiger, I will do what you ask."

"Yes, I am sure you will, I am sure you will," said Tiger, moving his tail slowly from side to side. "It is a little thing that I ask. Bring me Mr. Snake alive. Do you know Snake who lives down by the river, Mr. Anansi? Bring him to me alive and you can have the stories."

Tiger stopped speaking. He did not move his tail. He looked at Anansi and waited for him to speak. All the animals in the forest waited. Mr. Frog beneath the cool leaves, Mr. Parrot up in the tree, all watched Anansi. They were all ready to laugh at him.

"Tiger, I will do what you ask," said Anansi. At these words a great wave of laughter burst from the forest. The frogs and parrots laughed. Tiger laughed loudest of all, for how could feeble Anansi catch Snake alive?

Anansi went away. He heard the forest laughing at him from every side.

That was on Monday morning. Anansi sat before his house and thought of plan after plan. At last he hit upon one that could not fail. He would build a Calaban.

On Tuesday morning Anansi built a Calaban. He took a strong vine and made a noose. He hid the vine in the grass. Inside the noose he set some of the berries that Snake loved best. Then he waited. Soon Snake came up the path. He saw the berries and went toward them. He lay across the vine and ate the berries. Anansi pulled at the vine to tighten the noose, but Snake's body was too heavy. Anansi saw that the Calaban had failed.

Wednesday came. Anansi made a deep hole in the ground. He made the sides slippery with grease. In the bottom he put some of the bananas that Snake loved. Then he hid in the bush beside the road and waited.

Snake came crawling down the path toward the river. He was hungry and thirsty. He saw the bananas at the bottom of the hole. He saw that the sides of the hole were slippery. First he wrapped his tail tightly round the trunk of a tree, then he

reached down into the hole and ate the bananas. When he was finished he pulled himself up by his tail and crawled away. Anansi had lost his bananas and he had lost Snake, too.

Thursday morning came. Anansi made a Fly Up. Inside the trap he put an egg. Snake came down the path. He was happy this morning, so happy that he lifted his head and a third of his long body from the ground. He just lowered his head, took up the egg in his mouth, and never even touched the trap. The Fly Up could not catch Snake.

What was Anansi to do? Friday morning came. He sat and thought all day. It was no use.

Now it was Saturday morning. This was the last day. Anansi went for a walk down by the river. He passed by the hole where Snake lived. There was Snake, his body hidden in the hole, his head resting on the ground at the entrance to the hole. It was early morning. Snake was watching the sun rise above the mountains.

"Good morning, Anansi," said Snake.

"Good morning, Snake," said Anansi.

"Anansi, I am very angry with you. You have been trying to catch me all week. You set up a Fly Up to catch me. The day before you made a Slippery Hole for me. The day before that you made a Calaban. I have a good mind to kill you, Anansi."

"Ah, you are too clever, Snake," said Anansi. "You are much too clever. Yes, what you say is so. I tried to catch you, but I failed. Now I can never prove that you are the longest animal in the world, longer even than the bamboo tree."

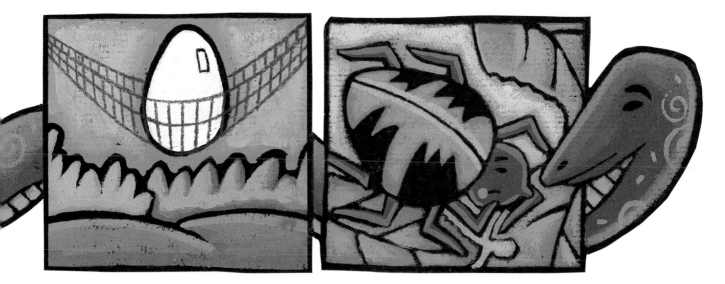

"Of course I am the longest of all animals," cried Snake. "I am much longer than the bamboo tree."

"What, longer than that bamboo tree across there?" asked Anansi.

"Of course I am," said Snake. "Look and see." Snake came out of the hole and stretched himself out at full length.

"Yes, you are very, very long," said Anansi, "but the bamboo tree is very long, too. Now that I look at you and at the bamboo tree I must say that the bamboo tree seems longer. But it's hard to say because it is further away."

"Well, bring it nearer," cried Snake. "Cut it down and put it beside me. You will soon see that I am much longer."

Anansi ran to the bamboo tree and cut it down. He placed it on the ground and cut off all its branches. Bush, bush, bush, bush! There it was, long and straight as a flagstaff.

"Now put it beside me," said Snake.

Anansi put the long bamboo tree down on the ground beside Snake. Then he said:

"Snake, when I go up to see where your head is, you will crawl up. When I go down to see where your tail is, you will crawl down. In that way you will always seem to be longer than the bamboo tree, which really is longer than you are."

"Tie my tail, then!" said Snake. "Tie my tail! I know that I am longer than the bamboo, whatever you say."

Anansi tied Snake's tail to the end of the bamboo. Then he ran up to the other end.

"Stretch, Snake, stretch, and we will see who is longer."

A crowd of animals was gathering round. Here was something better than a race. "Stretch, Snake, stretch," they called.

Snake stretched as hard as he could. Anansi tied him round his middle so that he should not slip back. Now one more try. Snake knew that if he stretched hard enough he would prove to be longer than the bamboo.

Anansi ran up to him. "Rest yourself for a little, Snake, and then stretch again. If you can stretch another fifteen centimetres you will be longer than the bamboo. Try your hardest. Stretch so that you even have to shut your eyes. Ready?"

"Yes," said Snake. Then Snake made a mighty effort. He stretched so hard that he had to squeeze his eyes shut.

"Hooray!" cried the animals. "You are winning, Snake. Just five centimetres more."

And at that moment Anansi tied Snake's head to the bamboo. There he was. At last he had caught Snake, all by himself.

The animals fell silent. Yes, there Snake was, all tied up, ready to be taken to Tiger. And feeble Anansi had done this. They could laugh at him no more.

And never again did Tiger dare to call these stories by his name. They were Anansi stories for ever after, from that day to this.

ABOUT THE AUTHOR PHILIP SHERLOCK

Sir Philip Sherlock was born in Jamaica and grew up in a remote village on that island. He has travelled a great deal in Western Europe and North and Central America, and is a respected scholar, historian, and writer. He lives in Kingston, Jamaica.

A World of Tricksters

by Elma Schemenauer
Illustrated by Susan Todd

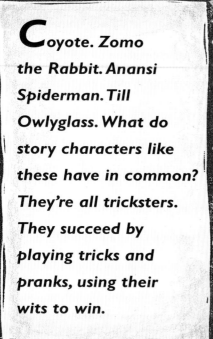

Coyote. Zomo the Rabbit. Anansi Spiderman. Till Owlyglass. What do story characters like these have in common? They're all tricksters. They succeed by playing tricks and pranks, using their wits to win.

Many trickster tales are very old. They began long before people had television, computer games, CD-ROMs, or even books. During the long evenings by the flickering firelight, storytellers told trickster tales. Eager listeners acted them out, sang songs about them, and retold them again and again.

What Makes a Trickster?

Tricksters are surely some of the strangest story characters people have ever invented. Many of them are animals, or at least are animals *sometimes*. For many tricky tricksters have magical powers that allow them to turn from animals to human and back again. For example, Anansi Spiderman is sometimes a spider living among the animals, and sometimes a human man living in a village. Whatever shape he is, he is always full of mischief.

Another interesting thing about tricksters is that they are almost always small and weak, while their opponents are big and strong. People love to root for an underdog, so it's easy to see why they enjoy seeing a clever trickster like Hare use his wits to befuddle a fierce opponent like Tiger.

Even so, tricksters don't always have the last laugh. Their weaknesses sometimes trip them up. In one Anansi tale, the clever Spiderman tricks poor Tortoise out of his dinner, but ends up tricked himself. That's one thing that makes the stories so interesting—you're never quite sure what's going to happen in the end!

Tricksters are complicated characters, and some of their character traits seem to contradict each other. Raven, the great trickster of the Aboriginal Peoples of the Northwest Coast, is often noble and wise. He brings light to the world, makes the rivers run, and helps humankind. Yet Raven is also sneaky, selfish, and very greedy. He's always trying to trick people into feeding him, and that gets him into plenty of trouble.

A Who's Who of Tricksters

Tricksters are found all over the world. In Hawaii, Maui is a famous trickster who takes the shapes of many different animals to get away with mischief. He also has great powers—once he slowed down the sun to make the days longer. In Japan, people tell tales about Tanuki the Badger, who once turned himself into a teakettle as a prank, and got singed when someone put him on the fire.

In India, Monkey is a hero who helps King Rama rescue his wife from an evil demon—but he can't resist playing tricks along the way. In Africa, people tell how Zomo the Rabbit got wisdom by using tricks to do three impossible tasks.

Europe has many trickster figures too. In Russia and many other northern lands, Fox almost always outwits his enemies by his cleverness. In Germany and the Netherlands, Till Owlyglass is the favorite trickster. Till played many merry pranks on solemn, stuffy folks. People got so angry at him that some vowed to put an end to him. According to one story, they did, but in other versions Till survived to make more mischief.

In Central America and North America, one of the best-loved tricksters is Coyote. A favorite Mexican tale tells how the great trickster was tricked himself by the little lamb Borreguita. She saved herself from being eaten by telling him the moon's reflection in the pond was a giant piece of tasty cheese. Coyote got very wet finding out it wasn't!

Travelling Tricksters

Some tricksters have crossed oceans and travelled thousands of kilometres with their storytellers to find new homes, sometimes adapting their names as they go. Anansi Spiderman is one of the greatest travellers. He came originally from Ghana, in western Africa, where he was known as Ananse. From there, Black storytellers brought him to the Caribbean, and from there he found his way to Central America, So the clever Spider is known by all sorts of names—Ananse, Anansi, Anancy, and Nancy.

Here's another interesting thing. The Sioux and Cheyenne peoples of the Great Plains tell tales of a trickster called Iktomi, who is magical, but who is also a mischief-maker who is always getting into trouble. In their languages, "Iktomi" means "spider."

Rabbit is another traveller. He started out as Zomo the Rabbit in West Africa, and became Br'er Rabbit in North America when Black peoples brought there as slaves changed the stories of their homelands to fit their new surroundings. In other lands, such as Korea, Hare is a famous trickster. Is he the same character as Rabbit? Nobody knows for sure. All we know is that the traits associated with certain animals seem to be similar in a variety of cultures.

Why Trickster Tales Are Told

Some trickster tales are actually *myths*—stories that explain how the world came to be. This is especially true in North America, where the Aboriginal Peoples explained the world around them through the adventures of great tricksters such as Raven, Coyote, and Glooscap.

Trickster tales carry other messages, too. The conflict between the characters in the tales is what makes them exciting. Yet many of the tales show that conflicts can be resolved in non-violent ways. For example, in one story, Br'er Rabbit persuades Br'er Fox not to kill him for playing tricks. Instead, he gets his opponent to "punish" him by throwing him into the briar patch—which is right where Br'er Rabbit wants to be!

How tricksters and their opponents behave in the stories is important in other ways, too. That's because the stories teach the values of the people who tell them—what they like, fear, honor, or scorn. When the trickster Nanabozho greedily cooks far more ducks than he needs for his dinner, Wolf comes along and gobbles them all up. Nanabozho goes hungry, and that is exactly the right punishment for his greed.

So, storytellers pass all kinds of important messages to their listeners or readers through trickster tales. That's probably not the only reason people pay attention, though. Trickster tales are also lots of fun!

ABOUT THE AUTHOR

ELMA SCHEMENAUER

Elma Schemenauer has written many books for young readers, including *Jacob Jacobs Gets Up Early, Yesterstories,* and *Special Canadian Communities.* Before starting to write books, Elma was a teacher in Nova Scotia, Montana, and Saskatchewan. She likes animals, travel, and adventure.

How Raven freed the Moon

by Anne Cameron
Illustrated by Luc Melanson

Raven is the trickster.
She never uses force.
She uses her wits and her magic, and sometimes she outsmarts herself.

Raven is often good, sometimes bad; Raven is always beautiful.

Above all else, Raven loves beautiful things, especially bright, shiny things.

One day, Raven heard the people talking about an old fisherwoman and her daughter who lived on an island far to the north and had a round, bright, shiny thing called Moon which they kept in a beautiful carved cedar box, locked away from those who might want to steal it.

Raven wanted the moon.

Raven flew all day in the bright sunlight. Heading north, she flew over the rivers and streams, over the mountains and valleys, over the trees and beach, searching for the old fisherwoman and her daughter, searching for the round, bright, shiny Moon.

Raven flew all night through the darkness. In the sky there were only pinpoints of light as the stars tried to light her way.

Finally, just when Raven thought she was too tired to go any further, she arrived at the house of the fisherwoman and her daughter.

Quickly, Raven used her magic. She turned herself into a lovely little baby girl, lay down by the door, and began to cry.

Inside the cedar log house the fisherwoman stirred restlessly. Then she sat up, rubbed her eyes, and looked around her house. Everything was exactly as it should be.

So she lay back down again.

Raven, who was no longer a bird, but a lovely little baby girl, took a deeper breath and cried even more loudly.

"What's that?" the fisherwoman demanded.

"It sounds like a baby," replied her daughter.

"There's no baby around here," the fisherwoman said firmly.

"Still," the daughter puzzled, "it does sound like a baby."

Raven could hear their voices. She took several deep breaths and howled at the top of her voice.

"My heavens!" the fisherwoman gasped. "It certainly does sound like a baby."

So they got out of bed, went to their door, opened it, and saw the most beautiful little baby girl they had ever seen. A little girl with coal black hair and shiny black eyes, crying and holding out her arms to be picked up and cuddled.

"Is that your baby?" the fisherwoman asked.

"No," her daughter answered. "No, it most certainly is not my baby."

"Then whose baby is it?" They stared down at the baby, who smiled at them and made soft cooing noises and appeared to be quite the most wonderful of babies.

"I think," the daughter smiled, picking up the baby and cuddling it gently, "I think she is our baby."

The daughter carried the baby (who was, of course, Raven) into the house and wrapped her in a nice warm blanket. "Oh, she has such cold hands and feet," she said.

"Of course she has," the fisherwoman replied sleepily. "And she's probably hungry. No baby should sleep outside at night. Anything might happen to her. If you want to keep that baby, you'll have to feed her, keep her warm, dry, and clean; and above all keep her quiet. I am an old woman and I need my sleep. I work very hard and need my rest." Yawning and scolding, the old fisherwoman went back to her bed and fell asleep.

The daughter gave the baby (who was, of course, Raven) some nice smoked fish to eat. "My," she said, "this baby certainly does eat a lot." She did not know the hungry baby was really Raven. She probably would not have believed it if anyone had told her.

Nobody ever expects magic to happen.

The lovely little baby girl smiled and cuddled, laughed and gurgled, and ate a great deal. The daughter of the old fisherwoman began to get very sleepy, for it was, after all, the middle of the night. She made a bed for the beautiful baby girl, tucked her in, kissed her good night, and went to her own bed.

No sooner had she pulled up her covers and closed her eyes than the baby began to cry!

"What is that noise?" the old fisherwoman demanded, sitting up in bed and looking around her with fierce eyes.

"It's our baby," the daughter said sleepily.

"What's the matter with her?"

"I don't know."

"She's crying."

"Yes, mother, she certainly is crying."

"Well, make her stop!" the fisherwoman insisted. "I have a big day ahead of me, and I won't be able to do my work if I don't get enough sleep."

The baby (who was, of course, Raven) continued to cry.

So the daughter got out of bed, went over, picked up the baby, and sang her a song.

The baby did not go back to sleep, but the old fisherwoman did. And soon, the song made the daughter sleepy, too. So, once again, she tucked the beautiful little baby girl into her bed, kissed her goodnight, and went back to her own bed to try to get some sleep.

But no sooner had she pulled up her covers and closed her eyes than that baby (Raven) began to cry. Again.

Before the fisherwoman could even ask what was wrong, the daughter was out of bed and over to the baby.

She tickled the baby's toes.

She smiled.

She sang.

She tried everything she knew.

And that baby cried.

"Oh, for heaven's sake," snapped the old fisherwoman, "this has just got to stop."

"What should I do? She has eaten, she is warm and dry, and still she cries and cries and cries."

"Maybe," the old fisherwoman sighed, "you should find something for her to play with."

At this, the baby (who was, of course, Raven) laughed happily and reached out her arms for the carved wooden box. "OH NO, baby!" the daughter said quickly, "you mustn't touch that."

The baby opened her lovely little mouth, took a very deep breath and ROARED.

"Oh, my!" the daughter gasped.

"What's that!" the old fisherwoman demanded, almost jumping out of her skin.

"She wants the carved box in which we keep . . . you know," the daughter said.

"Well, she can't have that!" the old fisherwoman grumbled. "It's no toy for a baby."

The baby howled louder.

She sobbed.

She wailed.

"Wah wah wah ah-wah!"

"I can't stand any more of this!" the old fisherwoman said. "Let her at least look at the box. But she mustn't hold it herself, she'll drop it."

"Yes, Mother," the daughter agreed.

The daughter got the beautiful carved cedar box and put it where the baby could see it.

"Goo goo," smiled the baby, and laughed happily.

"Don't touch it, baby," the daughter sighed with relief. "You may look at it, but you mustn't touch it."

The baby (who was, of course, Raven) lay on her side staring at the box, making soft happy noises.

The soft happy noises made the daughter very sleepy. She yawned and yawned and rubbed her eyes. She tried to stay awake.

But she fell asleep.

The baby (who was, of course, really Raven) crawled over to the carved cedar box, and carefully lifted the lid.

Inside, on a piece of soft otter fur, lay Moon.

The baby reached out, took the moon in her hand, and gazed at its beauty.

She knew she wanted to keep Moon.

The bright light from the moon shone on the face of the old fisherwoman and wakened her.

"That's not baby!" she shouted. "That's RAVEN!"

"RAVEN!" the daughter exclaimed, waking.

And sure enough, there in their little house was Raven, holding Moon under one large, black wing.

"Get the Moon!" the old fisherwoman cried, jumping from her bed and racing after Raven.

"I'll catch her!" the daughter shouted.

But of course she didn't.

The old fisherwoman and her daughter chased Raven around the house, knocking over furniture, tripping over each other, getting more and more angry and upset.

"Caw, caw, caw!" mocked Raven. "You can't catch me! Caw, caw, caw!"

And Raven put Moon in her beak and flew up the smokehole in the roof.

"Caw, caw, caw!" Raven laughed. "It's mine, all mine." She flew south, toward her home, with Moon in her beak.

Through the night, which was lighted by the Moon in her beak and no longer pitch black, Raven flew swiftly over trees and meadows, rivers and streams.

But Moon is not a pebble off the beach. Moon is not a huckleberry. Moon is very large and very heavy.

Soon Raven could no longer fly with Moon in her beak. She was too tired. She was so tired she almost dropped Moon into the ocean waves.

Raven knew she would never make it over the mountains with Moon in her beak.

So Raven tossed the Moon up, up, up into the sky as high as she could and Moon caught on a corner of a cloud.

So high did Moon go and so brightly did it light up the sky that the old fisherwoman and her daughter saw it in their land far to the north.

"Look!" said the daughter, "look up there in the sky . . ."

"That's our Moon," said the fisherwoman.

Her daughter smiled, and shrugged. "But look at it," she said. "Moon looks much better up in the sky than it ever looked in that box."

ABOUT THE AUTHOR — ANNE CAMERON

Anne Cameron is the author of nearly thirty books of fiction, poems, legends, and children's books, including *How the Loon Lost Her Voice*, *Raven Returns the Water*, and *Orca's Song*. Anne also writes scripts for TV, film, and radio, and has recently released an audio tape for children, *Loon and Raven Tales*. She lives on a farm near Powell River, BC.

The Greedy Butchers

by Ian Serraillier
Illustrated by Margo Thompson

1. The Road to Nottingham

Come to me, all you young gallants, O come
   From town and meadow and wood!
If you listen a while, I'll sing you a song
   Of an archer, bold Robin Hood.

Once, as he walked in the merry greenwood,
   It chanced bold Robin did see
A butcher astride a bonny fine mare,
   And riding to market was he.

"Good morrow, good fellow," said Robin Hood.
   "What carry you there in your pack?
And tell me your trade and where you dwell—
   I trust you'll safely get back."

The butcher he answered Robin Hood,
   "What matters it where I dwell?
For a butcher am I, and to Nottingham town
   I am going, my meat to sell."

"What is the price of your mare?" said Robin.
   "Tell me, I'm eager to learn.
And what is the price of your meat, for I wish
   As a butcher my living to earn?"

"The price of my meat?" the butcher replied.
   "I can reckon that up in a minute . . .
Four shillings, good sir, is none too dear—
   And a bonny fine mare to go with it."

"Four guineas I'll give you," said Robin Hood,
   "Four guineas in gold I'll pay."
They counted their money, exchanged their clothes,
   And each rode off on his way.

2. The Market

So Robin Hood rode to Nottingham town
 On the butcher's bonny fine mare.
Though others might charge too dear for their meat,
 He vowed *his* price should be fair.

But the sheriff he was in league with these rogues,
 He too was a twister and cheat.
What cared he if the price was too high
 And the poor could buy no meat?

In their stalls the butchers opened their meat,
 On dish and platter displayed;
For many a year they'd swindled the poor,
 But Robin was new to the trade.

Yet not a bite, not a morsel they sold,
 While bountiful Robin did well:
He sold more meat for one penny piece
 Than the rest for three pennies could sell.

Those villainous butchers fell back, amazed;
 The sheriff he scratched his head.
"If this fellow continues in trade, we'll starve.
 We must teach him a lesson," they said.

The butchers stepped over to Robin, resolved
    That some pretty trick should be played.
"Good brother," said one, "will you join us for dinner?
    Do come—we are all in the trade."

"Such offers," said Robin, "I never refuse."
    And to dinner they hurried apace.
The sheriff sat down at the head of the table,
    And asked Robin Hood to say grace.

"And when you've said grace, you shall sit at my side
    And we'll drink to success and long life."
"I'll gladly say grace," said bold Robin Hood,
    "If I may sit next to your wife."

The sheriff agreed. "God bless us!" said Robin.
    "Good appetite! Drink your fill!
Though five pounds and more it cost me in gold,
    I vow that I'll settle the bill."

"This fellow is crazy," the butchers declared.
    Said the sheriff, "He's due for a fall.
He has sold all his land for silver and gold,
    And means to squander it all."

"May he squander it all in this house," said the butchers,
    "And part with it, quick as can be!"
"Be patient! I've thought of a trick," said the sheriff.
    "I beg you to leave it to me."

 3. Into the Greenwood

Said the sheriff to Robin, "What have you to sell?
    Any cattle or hornéd beast?"
"Indeed, I have plenty, good master sheriff,
    Two or three hundred at least."

The sheriff saddled his dapple-grey,
    With three hundred pound in gold;
And away he went with bold Robin Hood,
    His hornéd beasts to behold.

By hill and furrow and field they rode,
    To the forest of merry Sherwood.
"O, Heaven forbid," the sheriff exclaimed,
    "That we meet with Robin Hood!"

"Why do you tremble and shake?" said Robin.
    "You should trust, good sir, in me.
With my brave longbow and arrows I'll show
    I can shoot as straight as he."

When to a leafy hollow they came,
    Bold Robin chanced to spy
A hundred head of good red deer
    Through the trees come tripping by.

"Good master sheriff, how like you my beasts?
    They're sleek—and see how they race!"
"I tell you, good fellow, I'd rather go home—
    I don't like the look on your face."

Then Robin Hood put his horn to his mouth,
    He blew blasts two and three—
And fifty bowmen with brave Little John
    Stood under the greenwood tree.

"What is your will?" then said Little John.
    "Good master, what must we do?"
"I have brought the sheriff of Nottingham town
    Today to have dinner with you."

"He is welcome indeed," said Little John.
    "I hope from his purse he will pay
Guineas and shillings to give to the poor,
    To gladden them many a day."

Robin Hood stripped the cloak from his back
    And laying it down on the ground,
He emptied the purse—in silver and gold
    He counted three hundred pound.

Then lo! through the greenwood the sheriff he led,
    Sitting glum on his old dapple-grey.
"Remember me, sir, to your lady at home!"
    Laughed Robin, and galloped away.

The Rajah's Rice

by David Barry
Illustrated by Donna Perrone

Once upon a time a long time ago, a girl named Chandra lived in a small village in India. Chandra loved elephants. She also loved numbers. So of course she loved all numbers to do with elephants: two tusks to polish on each elephant, eighteen toenails to clean, a hundred scrubs on a side at each bath. Chandra had many chances to think about elephant numbers because she had a special job: She was the bather of the Rajah's elephants.

Chandra liked other numbers, too. As she walked past rice paddies, muddy after the harvest, she counted the snowy egrets that flew above her.

She passed through the marketplace at the edge of the village and stopped to help the spice peddler count change.

When she joined her friends where they stood watching the Rajah's elephants parade through the town square, she remembered every elephant number she knew. Then she started thinking about rice.

It was rent collection day, and bags bulging with rice hung from the sides of the elephants.

No wonder the people looked sad. The Rajah had taken so much rice for himself that the whole village would be hungry.

But this was the way it had always been. For thousands of years the villagers had farmed the Rajah's land. For thousands of years, he had come with his elephants to take most of the rice harvest.

The whole thing made Chandra angry, but what could she do?

On the elephants' next bath day, Chandra packed up her equipment and walked over the fields to the palace. She was about to enter the gates when the guard stopped her.

"You cannot come in this morning, Elephant Bather. The elephants have taken sick."

Chandra peered through the bamboo gate into the elephant yard. There she could see her elephants lying on the ground as still as felled trees. No amount of calling, singing, or cooing made them so much as raise their heads.

Over the days that followed Chandra sat watch over her precious elephants. She was not allowed inside, so she waited at the gate, watching medical men from all across the land come to cure the elephants.

The first doctor sat on cushions in the courtyard and feasted; he ate eight meat pastries, ten chickpea dumplings, and twelve sand lobsters served on banana leaves at each meal. While he ate, the elephants got sicker.

Another doctor spent all day and most of the night in the elephant yard chanting and burning incense. The elephants got even sicker.

Seven more doctors came and went, but the elephants got still sicker.

One morning, the Rajah returned from a walk in the gardens to find Chandra at the gate, staring in at the elephants. "What are you doing here, Elephant Bather?" he asked.

"I worry about the elephants," she said. "I love them all and know them well. Maybe I can help them."

The Rajah thought for a moment. "Go ahead and try," he said. "I need those elephants. Without them, I will not be able to carry the rice to market on market day. If you can save them, you may choose your own reward."

The guard opened the gates, and Chandra and the Rajah walked in silence to the elephant yard. Chandra approached Misha, the Rajah's favorite elephant. She studied his feet: the nails, the pads, the cuticles. She studied his tusks and the eight molars deep inside his mouth. She studied the lips, the tongue, and the throat. She looked deep into his eyes.

When Chandra got to the first ear, she discovered a painful-looking infection inside the ear canal. The other ear was the same. So were the ears of the other elephants. Chandra cleaned their ears, sang the elephants a soothing song, and went home.

At dawn the next day, when Chandra returned, the elephants were walking unsteadily around their yard. They greeted her with joyful trumpeting.

The Rajah was overjoyed. He declared a festival day and invited everyone in the land to the palace.

The Rajah led Chandra to the ceremony room. Piled on a long

table, next to the Rajah's chessboard, was a glittering array of gold necklaces, brilliant sapphires and rubies, diamond brooches, bags of gold rupees, and other treasures.

The guests began to arrive, and soon the ceremony room was crowded with villagers.

"Name your reward, Elephant Bather," said the Rajah.

Chandra looked at the beautiful jewels on the table before her. She thought about her elephants and the hundreds of sacks of rice they carried away from the village each year. And then she noticed the chessboard.

"The villagers are hungry, Rajah," she began. "All I ask for is rice. If Your Majesty pleases, place two grains of rice on the first square of this chessboard. Place four grains of rice on the second square, eight on the next, and so on, doubling each pile of rice till the last square."

The villagers shook their heads sadly at Chandra's choice.

The Rajah was secretly delighted. A few piles of rice would certainly be far cheaper than his precious jewellery. "Honor her request," he boomed to his servants.

Two servants brought out a small bowl of rice and carefully placed two grains of rice on the first square of the board. They placed four grains of rice on the second square. Then eight on the third square, sixteen on the fourth square, thirty-two on the fifth square, sixty-four on the sixth square, 128 on the seventh square, and finally 256 grains of rice on the eighth square at the end of the row.

Several servants snickered at Chandra's foolishness, for although the 256 grains of rice filled the eighth square completely, they amounted to only a single teaspoon of rice.

At the first square of the second row, the servants stood awkwardly, not knowing how to count out the rice. The next number was 512, but that was too high to count quickly, and besides, it was too many grains of rice to fit on one square of the chessboard.

Chandra started to explain. "Since you had one teaspoon of rice at the end of the first row, why not just put two teaspoons—"

But the Rajah cut in. "Just keep doubling the rice," he ordered. "You don't need to count every grain."

So the servants put two teaspoons of rice into a bowl for the first square of the second row. For the second square, they put four teaspoons of rice in the bowl. Then eight teaspoons of rice for the third square, and so continued, doubling the number of teaspoons each square.

The eighth square on the second row needed 256 teaspoons of rice, which by itself filled another bowl.

On the third row, the servants started to count by teaspoons again, but the Rajah cut in. Showing off his knowledge of mathematics, he said, "If the sixteenth square takes one bowl of rice, then the seventeenth square takes two bowls of rice. You don't need to count by teaspoons anymore."

So the servants counted by bowls. Two bowlfuls for the first square, then four, then eight, then sixteen, and so on. The rice for the last square of the third row completely filled a large wheelbarrow.

Chandra's neighbors smiled at her. "Very nice," one of them said. "That would feed my family for a whole year."

As the servants worked through the fourth row, wheelbarrow by

wheelbarrow, the Rajah paced back and forth, his eyes wide in amazement. His servants gathered around him. "Shall we bring rice from your royal storehouses?" they asked.

"Of course," was the reply. "A Rajah never breaks a promise." The servants took the elephants and headed out to the first storehouse to get more rice.

By late afternoon, the Rajah had collapsed onto his couch. As his attendants fanned him with palm fronds, the servants started on the fifth row of the chessboard, and soon they were emptying entire storehouses into the courtyard.

Within several squares, rice poured from the windows of the palace and into the gardens beyond. By the middle of the fifth row, all of the Rajah's storehouses were empty.

He had run out of rice.

The Rajah struggled to his feet and ordered the rice to be loaded onto the elephants and taken to the village. Then he approached Chandra.

"Elephant Bather," he said to her, "I am out of rice and cannot fill the chessboard. Tell me what I can give yout to be released from my vow."

"You can give the people of the village the land they farm, and take only the rice you need for yourself," answered Chandra.

The Rajah gazed at the mountains of rice that filled his palace and gardens, then out beyond the gardens to the fields the villagers farmed, stretching as far as he could see. Then he looked back at Chandra, the elephant bather.

"It is done," he said.

That night the Rajah arrived in the village as Chandra and the other villagers prepared a celebration feast.

"Would you be so kind as to join me for a short walk, Chandra?" he asked. "I have a question for you."

As they strolled toward the village square, the Rajah spoke. "I am a very rich man, and it took all of the rice I owned to fill little more than one-half of the chessboard. How much rice would it have taken to fill the whole board?" he asked.

"If you had kept doubling the rice to the last square of the chessboard, all of India would be knee-deep in rice," said Chandra, and smiled.

ABOUT THE AUTHOR   DAVID BARRY

David Barry is a lawyer, softwear designer, and an inventor. On top of all that, he finds time to teach occasional math classes in an elementary school. He lives with his wife and three children in California. *The Rajah's Rice* is his first book.

Finn McCool

by May Lynch
Photographed by Gilbert Duclos

In this dramatization of an Irish tale, a giant named Cuhullin comes looking for Finn McCool. Finn and his wife, Una, have to think of a way to outwit Cuhullin.

CHARACTERS

Finn McCool
Una, his wife
Owen
John
Jamie   } their children
Meg
Celia
Grannie
Mrs. O'Malley
Mrs. Shane
Cuhullin

SETTING: *The interior of Finn McCool's cabin, on top of Knockmany Mountain, in Ireland.*

AT RISE: *UNA stands at a washtub, wringing out a piece of clothing. She places it on top of a basket of laundry at her feet. OWEN, JAMIE, and JOHN are sitting nearby.*

UNA: There! That's the last of my washing, and I must say it was a big one.

OWEN: I'll say it was. I carried six buckets of water up Knockmany Mountain this morning.

JOHN: And so did Jamie and I. We do it all the time.

OWEN: You didn't carry six buckets, John.

JAMIE: *(laughing)* No, Owen, but you spilled half of yours.

OWEN: I did not, Jamie McCool!

JAMIE: You did, too.

OWEN: *(loudly)* I did not!

UNA: Children! Stop that brawling and squalling. My, I'll be glad when your father, Finn McCool, finds us a spring up here near the house.

JOHN: He says that there's water right out there under those two rocks.

JAMIE: Yes, and he's going to move them someday.

OWEN: *(interrupting)* Someday! Someday! He keeps saying *someday*, but *someday* never comes.

UNA: Owen McCool, don't speak that way of your father. After all, the dear man is very busy and tired—and—and busy. *(MEG and CELIA enter.)*

CELIA: Mother! Mother! Guess what!

MEG: Grannie Owen and Mrs. O'Malley and Mrs. Shane are coming up Knockmany Mountain right now.

UNA: Your grannie hasn't been here in a long time. Put on the teakettle, Meg. Celia, dear, lay the cloth. And Owen, hang these things out on the line, like a good boy.

OWEN: I have to do *everything*.

JAMIE: I'll help you. Come on. *(He picks up basket of laundry. The two BOYS exit.)*

JOHN: I'll fix the fire. *(UNA and the GIRLS tidy up the room, as JOHN kneels at fireplace.)*

CELIA: *(at window)* Here they are. I see them coming up the path.

JOHN: *(opening the door)* Welcome, Grannie. Good day, Mrs. Shane. Good health to you, Mrs. O'Malley.

GRANNIE, MRS. O'MALLEY, and MRS. SHANE enter. All exchange greetings. The GIRLS kiss GRANNIE.

GRANNIE: Well, I must say, Knockmany Mountain gets steeper every year. I'm puffing from that long walk.

MRS. O'MALLEY: I am, too. And that wind gets stronger and stronger.

MRS. SHANE: Una, however do you manage in winter when that cold wind howls and blows and screams? Aren't you afraid to be up here?

UNA: (laughing) No, indeed. Finn McCool wouldn't live anywhere else in the world. (LADIES glance at each other with knowing looks.)

GRANNIE: Where is Finn today?

JOHN: He's somewhere about. He's busy, I guess.

UNA: He's such a busy man, you know.

MRS. SHANE: It's too bad he's too busy to find a spring up here. Those poor lads of yours shouldn't have to carry water all the way up the mountain.

JOHN: We really like to do that, Mrs. Shane. Besides, our father says that someday he is going to let my brothers and me help him split open those rocks out there. There's water under them. (LADIES shake their heads.)

MEG: Grannie, Mother, Mrs. O'Malley, Mrs. Shane, do sit down and have a cup of tea. (LADIES sit, as GIRLS serve them tea and pass a plate of cakes.)

GRANNIE: It's good to see you, Una. Since Finn built this house on top of the world, we seldom get together.

MRS. SHANE: Is it true, Una, that Finn came up here to get away from Cuhullin?

UNA: Goodness, no.

JOHN: Who is Cuhullin?

MRS. O'MALLEY: (quickly) Nobody important, John.

MRS. SHANE: Nobody important? He's a giant. That's who he is.

JOHN: Finn McCool, our father, is a giant, too.

MRS. SHANE: Oh, but Cuhullin is very strong. There's not a man so strong within a hundred miles of our town of Dungannon.

GRANNIE: Except maybe my son-in-law, Finn McCool.

MRS. SHANE: The talk around Dungannon right now is that Cuhullin once stamped his foot and all of Ireland shook and trembled.

JOHN: Why would he do that?

MRS. SHANE: To show that he had beaten every single giant in Ireland except Finn McCool, whom he can't find.

MRS. O'MALLEY: (nervously) I don't like to frighten you, Una, but there is talk in town that Cuhullin is on his way here to find Finn.

GRANNIE: But there's nothing to be afraid of, Una. You can all come down to my cottage and hide until Cuhullin goes away.

MRS. SHANE: Yes, you'd better.

MRS. O'MALLEY: Get the children and Finn right away, Una. My Mr. O'Malley heard only this morning that Cuhullin was thundering toward Dungannon.

MRS. SHANE: They say he'll stamp Finn into pancakes when he finds him.

JOHN: But why?

GRANNIE: It's an old story, John. Finn used to brag about how much stronger he was than Cuhullin. Of course, Cuhullin heard about it and he began to look for Finn McCool.

MRS. O'MALLEY: And he's never found him. Come, Una. Come with us.

UNA: Why, we have nothing to be afraid of. Finn will take care of us.

LADIES: *(ad lib; excitedly)* Please come right away. We're frightened. *(etc.)*

UNA: No, we'll be perfectly safe. *(Thinks for a moment.)* But I just remembered I must do some baking.

JOHN: You just did your week's baking, Mother. *(UNA starts to mix flour and salt in a bowl, as GRANNIE and other LADIES rise.)*

UNA: Did I indeed, John? *(to LADIES)* Must you go so soon, ladies? *(They nod and start toward door.)* Finn will be very sorry he wasn't here to see you. Come again soon.

GRANNIE: We will, Una. *(aside:)* Poor Finn will be no more. Poor Finn McCool. *(They exit.)*

CELIA: Mother, is it true what they said about Cuhullin? *(UNA shrugs and continues mixing.)*

UNA: *(to herself)* I need some iron skillets. *(Picks up two skillets.)* Here they are.

MEG: I'm scared, Mother.

UNA: *(to herself)* One bite of bread with a skillet in it will take care of Cuhullin. *(She starts to cover the skillets with dough. FINN enters.)*

FINN: I'm a dead man. I've been to Dungannon, and the giant Cuhullin is on his way to town looking for me. He told somebody he'd squeeze me into a sausage.

GIRLS: Is he big?

FINN: Big he is. Too big for me to handle. And *I'm* too big to hide from him.

UNA: You leave everything to me, Finn. I'll handle Cuhullin. Meg, give your father that old long nightdress of mine and find the baby's bonnet in the drawer. *(to FINN)* And *you* put on the nightdress and the bonnet and hide in that bed over there. *(She puts bread into oven. MEG exits.)*

FINN: Right here. Hide here in the open? *(UNA nods her head. He exits and returns wearing a long white nightgown and a bonnet. He climbs into bed, as MEG re-enters.)*

UNA: Girls, get Jamie and Owen and gather lots of kindling. Then build a great big fire right on the very tip of Knockmany Mountain.

CELIA: But a fire on the mountain means that we are welcoming a stranger. The only stranger is—is Cuhullin.

MEG: I'm too scared to move.

UNA: Go! Get your brothers to help you. *(to JOHN)* You, son, stand where the wind will carry your whistle. As soon as you see Cuhullin coming up the mountain, you must let out your long, loud whistle.

FINN: Ooooh! Ooooh! I'm scared out of my wits. Cuhullin will make a grease spot of me. He'll chew my darling children up alive and carry off my good wife.

UNA: Nonsense! You just listen to my plan. I've already made bread Cuhullin will never forget, and now if I take a cobblestone and make it look like a cheese—*(She sits on edge of bed and whispers in FINN'S ear. Both of them burst out into loud laughter. She whispers again, pointing to the oven. Loud whistle is heard.)* Cuhullin is coming! *(She pulls the covers around FINN.)* Now keep the bonnet on and remember who you are! *(She hands him a stone and a round cheese from the table.)* Now, don't roll on this cheese. *(A loud banging at the door is heard.)*

CUHULLIN: *(shouting from offstage)* Is this where you live, Finn McCool? Open up, if you're a man. *(UNA opens the door, looks surprised.)*

UNA: Well, I wondered if I heard someone at the door. It's so windy I don't always hear people knocking. Come in, stranger. Welcome.

CUHULLIN: *(entering)* Does Finn McCool live here?

UNA: *(sweetly)* He does, indeed.

CUHULLIN: Is he home?

UNA: Dear me, no! He left here an hour ago. Somebody said a giant named Cuhullin was down in Dungannon looking for him. Finn went right down to make pudding out of him.

CUHULLIN: Mm-m-m.

UNA: Did you ever hear of Cuhullin, poor thing?

CUHULLIN: That's me.

UNA: Oh, you poor man. Finn is in a terrible temper. Don't let him find you.

CUHULLIN: I've been wanting to meet him for years. I notice he doesn't let *me* find *him*.

UNA: Well, wait for him then. But don't say I didn't warn you.

CUHULLIN: I'll wait.

UNA: Don't be nervous. Here, to keep yourself from being scared, and while you're waiting, would you do me a favor? *(He nods.)* Would you turn the house around? Finn always turns it around in the fall when the wind blows at the door. It makes it warmer in winter.

CUHULLIN: Turn the house? Nothing easier. *(He exits. A loud noise is heard from offstage. UNA goes to the door. FINN groans.)*

UNA: *(calling)* That's better. Thank you very much. Now, would you do something else? Finn has been meaning to pull those rocks apart and find us a spring, but he hurried off, and I do need water. *(She steps back toward FINN as a loud crash is heard.)* Good heavens! He pulled apart those rocks with his bare hands and made a spring! *(FINN groans. CUHULLIN enters.)*

CUHULLIN: What now?

UNA: That's a good little job finished. Now you come and have a bite to eat. Even though you think Finn is your enemy, he would want me to be kind to anyone in our home. Here's a cup of tea and I have some hot bread right in the oven. *(She takes out loaves of bread. CUHULLIN bites into the bread.)*

CUHULLIN: Blood and thunder! I just broke my two front teeth. What did you give me to eat, woman?

UNA: Only what Finn always eats. He and our little child in the bed have these biscuits all the time. *(She indicates the bed.)* Try another one.

CUHULLIN: Jumping shamrocks. My teeth are ruined. Take this stuff away. What a toothache! *(holds jaw)*

FINN: *(in a deep voice)* Give me something to eat. I'm hungry! *(UNA takes a loaf of bread to FINN, and he pretends to eat it.)* Yum!

CUHULLIN: *(amazed)* I'd like to see that child. He must be some boy!

UNA: Get up, dearie, and show the man that you're Finn's little son.

FINN: *(jumping out of bed)* Are you strong like my father?

CUHULLIN: Toads and snakes! What a gigantic child!

FINN: Are you strong? Can you squeeze water from a stone? My father can, and so can I. *(He hands white stone to CUHULLIN, who squeezes it.)* Ah, you can't do it. *(FINN takes stone, throws it on bed, then picks up cheese, unseen by CUHULLIN, and squeezes it until water drips from it.)* My father, Finn McCool, taught me to do that. He can stamp a man to pancakes.

UNA: Into bed, son. You'll never grow strong and big like your father if you don't get your rest.

CUHULLIN: *(nervously)* I think I'd better go. I never saw the likes of that child. What must his father be like!

FINN: Will Father hurt that little man, Mother?

UNA: No, dearie. *(to CUHULLIN)* You are the lucky one that Finn isn't home. That temper of his! *(CUHULLIN exits, running. FINN and UNA laugh. The CHILDREN come running in.)*

MEG: Mother, what did you do to Cuhullin?

JOHN: He was holding his jaw and crying about a toothache.

OWEN: I heard him muttering about pancakes and a baby giant.

JAMIE: I watched from the bushes. He pulled those rocks apart one—two—three. And now we have a spring.

UNA: And he turned the house around. It's warmer already.

MEG: How did you do it, Mother?

FINN: Ah, your mother is a clever woman. She makes rocks out of cheese.

UNA: Your father fooled him. Cuhullin tried to squeeze water from a rock, but Finn squeezed water from *cheese.* Cuhullin never knew the difference.

FINN: And she put iron skillets into her bread and served them for biscuits.

UNA: But your father fooled him. He just nibbled around the crust.

OWEN: Why are you wearing that silly outfit, Father?

UNA: You should have seen how your father fooled him, pretending he was a baby giant. *(All laugh.)*

FINN: Now if somebody will help me out of this nightgown, I'll lie down and have a rest. A busy man like me gets very tired. *(Curtain.)*

The Ideas Peddler

by Sarah Ellis
Illustrated by Joe Weissmann

T his story took place very long ago or very far away or possibly both. It concerns a peddler and it happened in Aberbog, a tidy, organized, and prosperous town by the sea.

Every year in the fall there was a fair in town, and peddlers came from all around to sell their wares—boots and bells, spices and cloth, pots, knives, ribbons, perfume, pancake flippers, lotions, and liniments. The peddlers would sit in the market square on pieces of carpet with their merchandise piled all around them.

But one year a new peddler arrived and, unlike the others, sat down on his carpet with nothing at all. Now this was a town where people didn't ask many questions, so he sat there in silence for a long time. Finally a young woman named Sophie got very curious and came over to ask what he was selling. "Ideas," he replied. "I'm an ideas peddler."

Sophie wrinkled her nose. "Who would *buy* an idea?"

"Well," said the peddler, "they are bought by people whose ideas are worn out or moldy or out of style. They are bought by people who have used up their whole supply."

"How much do they cost?" asked Sophie.

"Depends on the type. The most expensive are thoughts, and they cost one night's lodging. The cheapest are whims, and they cost one apple. In between are concepts, plans, opinions, impressions, notions, and fancies."

By now Sophie was really interested, so she ran to the fruit stall and came back with an apple. "I'd like a whim, please."

The peddler pocketed the apple and said, "Here's a top-quality whim. If you glue little pieces of metal to the soles of your shoes you can make music when you dance."

"But I don't like dancing," protested Sophie.

"Oh, that's all right," said the peddler. "You don't have to do it. It's just an idea after all—some words to keep in your head." Sophie wandered away looking puzzled.

Nobody else bought an idea that day, and the peddler spent a hungry night in the open air. But the next day he fared better.

Mary the baker arrived in the early morning with a fresh loaf to buy an impression. The peddler looked up at the hills behind the town where the mist was just starting to burn off and said, "The hill in the middle is a giant carrot pudding just out of the oven."

Perkins and Snik, twin brothers who were fishermen, got together to buy a notion about the sea. When the peddler told them about tiny fish shaped like horses that swim upright through the waves, they were delighted and went off chuckling and hitting each other on the back.

From then on there was a steady stream of customers. Mind you, not all were completely satisfied. Jones the farmer, rich and grumpy, wanted a plan. The peddler suggested that he knit little sweaters to keep his pumpkins warm at night. "But," sputtered Jones, "men don't knit!" The peddler replied that there was no reason at all why men shouldn't knit, and then he charged Jones extra for an opinion.

Soon people were walking around town with little half smiles on their faces, murmuring such things as "Drawer spelled backward is reward," "If there were eight days in the week, we could have more holidays," or "Maybe the tide doesn't go out, maybe the land pulls back."

Children were especially fond of the peddler, and they visited him at the end of the day when he was known to give out free samples of notions and fancies, such as trolls living under bridges and using a bag of water for a bed.

Meanwhile the peddler was doing well. He was earning three good meals a day, a roof over his head at night, and he even had new soles on his boots. All would have been fine, if the mayor had not wandered by one day and noticed the peddler sitting in the market with a line of customers and no merchandise in sight. The mayor pushed to the front of the line. "What are you doing here? What are you selling?" he asked.

When the peddler told him about ideas, the mayor looked confused and then, because he didn't like being confused, he got angry.

"Where do you get these ideas?" he asked.

"I make them," replied the peddler.

"Sounds like you make them *up*."

"Up, down, sideways, via, and through," said the peddler with a faraway look.

By this time the mayor felt he was losing ground, and he turned around to glare at the crowd of people who were beginning to giggle.

"All right," he said, "let's have a look at one of these so-called ideas."

"Thought, concept, plan, opinion, impression, notion, fancy, or whim?" inquired the peddler.

"Give me a whim," said the mayor, who was totally lost by this time.

"Well," said the peddler, "if on a sunny day you hold your hand like this, near a wall, you can make a shadow that looks like a duck."

The mayor turned slightly purple. He opened and closed his mouth like a fish. "A duck! What good is that? What's it *for?* What use are these ideas?"

The peddler spoke very quietly. "The use of them is fresh air for the brain. They make you stop and smile and say to yourself, Gee whillikers! I never thought of that before."

"That's nonsense," said the mayor.

"Not actually," replied the peddler. "Where I come from, nonsense is sold by the nonsense peddler. He has all kinds of nonsense—absurdity, folly, trash, moonshine, twaddle, drivel, claptrap, bosh, balderdash, gobbledegook—"

"QUIET!" roared the mayor. "Aberbog will not stand for this insolence. You will hear from me tomorrow." And he turned on his heel and stamped off.

The next morning a special meeting of the town council was called, and the mayor announced, "We have to do something about that ideas peddler down at the market. He is dangerous." The counsellors knew that it wasn't a good thing to disagree with the mayor, so they all supported him wholeheartedly.

"Yes," said one, "new ideas are hazardous and untidy."

Soon there was a chorus of voices: "New ideas make people unhappy."

"Ideas are noisy."

"They have lumps."

"They don't match."

"They collect dust."

"They are expensive."

"They aren't natural."

"They shed."

"They hurt your brain."

"They cause allergies."

The mayor smiled. "So what should we do with the ideas peddler?"

"Run him out of town," yelled the counsellors.

"That's it," said the mayor. "Fine him, then run him out of town."

So the policeman was called, but by the time he went to find the peddler, the peddler had disappeared—disappeared without a trace. Nobody knew where he had gone and nobody in Aberbog ever saw him again.

But the damage was done. People had started thinking of their own new ideas, and they couldn't seem to stop. Everywhere you looked, people were pondering, musing, reflecting.

When the mayor objected, the people persuaded him to move to the next town, and Aberbog managed with no mayor at all.

And with all those ideas floating around, the town did become more untidy and disorganized. It also wasn't quite as prosperous. But it was a lot more fun to live there.

ABOUT THE AUTHOR SARAH ELLIS

Sarah Ellis likes reading, writing, and talking about books. She plays mix-and-match with these pleasures in her various jobs as librarian, university lecturer, book reviewer, storyteller, and writer for children. She lives in Vancouver, where she sometimes takes her nose out of a book to garden, cross-country ski, and have people for dinner. Her most recent enthusiasm is long-distance walking.

Old Wizard

Old Wizard was the wisest person in the world. He had a tremendous bucket of wisdom that he didn't share. A little boy named Oliver wanted the world to have some so he thought of a plan.

"Old Wizard, you may be smart but you're not strong," said Oliver.

"Yes I am!" Old Wizard said, insulted.

"You probably couldn't even move your bucket a millimetre!"

"I could so!"

"Show me."

"Fine."

Old Wizard pushed the bucket with all his power and might. It tipped right over and wisdom spilled everywhere. It quickly spread all over the world, thanks to one small boy who had always had some.

Katie O'Leary
Grade 6

I like writing things that I make up myself more than writing true stories. I like doing stories in a tale mode so that I can use my imagination. I usually do my stories and poems on the computer so that I can fix mistakes and change things quickly.

Katie O'Leary

How Carrie Got Her Dog

Carrie wanted a dog, but her parents said she couldn't get one because it would be too much trouble to look after. So one morning Carrie said, "Let's not get a dog, because we'll have to walk it in the park all the time with all the other people who have dogs." And her mom said, "Hmmm." Then Carrie said, "And let's not get a dog because it will bark everytime someone comes to the house." And her dad said, "Hmmm."

The next morning her mom said they were going to get a dog because she thought getting exercise in the park and meeting new friends would be fun. Then her dad said they were getting a dog because it would be good for safety if it barked when people came to the house. So then Carrie said, "Well, OK, if you really want one."

Rachel Fraser
Age 11

Clever Doug

Doug has always had clever ways of doing things. But he had to, living with three older brothers. At night he would set his alarm clock ten minutes earlier than anyone else in his family. This would give him enough time to wake up and get his breakfast before his brothers came and ate all of the good cereal. This would also give him time to get in the shower before all the hot water was used up by the other five members of his family.

Doug had gotten so used to waking up at the same time every day that most of the time he didn't need his alarm clock any more.

One day when Doug woke up and looked over at his alarm clock, 12:00 was flashing on and off. There had been a power failure. Doug immediately got out of bed yelling "Wake up, everyone, we slept in." Rushing out of bed, Doug's entire family stumbled to get ready to go to work and to school. Checking to see just how long he had slept in, Doug's father looked over at a clock. It read 12:00. Realizing there had been a power failure he turned on the radio and heard "Good morning early birds, it's time for the 3:00 a.m. news". Doug's father just looked at Doug and laughed as he put his pyjamas back on and crawled back to bed.

Matthew Stokes
Age 11

Michael Stokes, age 13

The Painter Mouse

Josh Cherun, Grade 7

There was once a mouse who got tired of having a cat waiting outside his hole all the time. He was afraid of getting caught, and wasn't getting enough treats. So one night when the cat was sleeping he went into the basement and put some paint into a little cup. Then he drew about 20 holes on the wall that looked just like his hole. From then on the cat was mixed up and was never waiting outside the right hole!

Robert Armour
Age 10

The Mirror

by Pleasant DeSpain
Illustrated by Hélène Bouliane

A large family of farmers lived in the country. There was a young husband and wife in this family, and the husband had to go to town on business. His wife asked, "Will you buy me a comb for my hair?"

"Anything for you, dear wife," he replied.

Now the wife knew that her husband was absent-minded, and wanted him to remember the comb. A new moon shone in the sky that night, just a thin crescent of light. It was the perfect shape of the comb she desired. She said to him, "Look at the moon, husband. It is just like the comb I want. If you forget, look at the moon and you'll remember."

The young man was in town for weeks, and was completely occupied with business matters. Naturally, he forgot all about the comb. When it came time to return home, he happened to look up into the night sky. The moon was no longer the crescent shape of a comb, but rather a full round sphere of yellow light.

"What is it that I'm supposed to bring to my wife?" the young farmer asked himself. "Something shaped like the moon. . . ."

He went to a shopkeeper and said, "I want to buy something that is round like the moon, something my wife would like."

The shopkeeper looked around his shop and said, "This mirror is round. Your wife would like to see herself in it."

Mirrors were quite rare in Korea at this long-ago time, and the young husband had never seen one before. He bought it and walked the long road back to the farm. The moon was rising in the night sky when he arrived. He gave the mirror to his wife. She looked into the glass and saw the reflection of a pretty young woman.

"Eeehhh!" she cried. "I ask for a comb and my husband brings home a young woman."

Her mother was in the room, and she looked into the mirror. Of course she saw her own wrinkled face, and said, "Silly daughter, this is no young woman. This is an old and honorable woman. Perhaps it is his mother."

"You are wrong," the wife said. "It is a pretty *young* woman."

"No, you are wrong," the mother replied. "Look! She's a white-haired *old* woman!"

As the two women argued, a small boy who was eating a rice cake came into the room. He picked up the mirror and saw another boy eating a rice cake.

The boy thought that the stranger had stolen his food. "Return my rice cake!" he shouted. He raised his fist and shook it at the stranger. The stranger shook his fist right back. The boy was frightened and he began to cry.

The noise of the women arguing and the boy crying brought the grandfather running into the room. "What's wrong?" he asked.

The boy said that a stranger had stolen his rice cake. The grandfather became angry and said, "Show me the scoundrel. No one steals from my grandson and gets away with it!" He grabbed the mirror and saw an enraged old man with fire in his eyes.

"Listen old man," said Grandfather. "You should be ashamed of yourself for stealing from a boy. I'm going to teach you a lesson!"

He made a fist and punched his image in the glass.

The mirror crashed to the floor! Grandfather, grandmother, the boy, the wife, and the husband stared with amazement at the broken bits of glass scattered all over the room.

"I think the thief is gone," said the boy.

"And I think I'll let my wife do her own shopping from now on," said the husband.

"I'll get the broom," said Grandmother.

The wife stepped out on the porch and looked up at the night sky. It may have just been a cloud passing by, but it looked to her as though the moon winked!

ABOUT THE AUTHOR   PLEASANT DeSPAIN

Ever since he was in Grade Three, Pleasant DeSpain has liked to write and tell stories. When he was twenty-eight, he decided to become a professional storyteller. Pleasant tells and writes exciting tales from all around the world. In most of his stories, good wins over evil, and common sense wins over strength.

Simply Ridiculous

Retold by Virginia Davis
Illustrated by Russ Willms

In a village far, far away there lived a young man who was sometimes a little silly. One day his wife came to him and said, "Willy, we're going to have a child."

"Oh, wife," Willy cried happily, "what kind of child will we have?"

"Well, husband, I don't know," she replied.

"You don't know?" grumbled Willy. He thought for a time and said, "But I want to know now. I will go to see the Wise Old Man. He will tell me."

So Willy took a cow as a gift and went up the hills to the mountain of the Wise Old Man.

The old man saw him coming and called out, "Have you come to partake of my wisdom?"

"Yes," said Willy. "I need your help."

"Well, come in, sit down, and tell me your troubles."

So Willy did. He told how he had grown to be a young man and had fallen in love and married. Now he was to be a father. But his wife could not tell him what kind of child they would have, and he had come to the Wise Old Man to find out.

The old man smiled. "I think I can help," he said.

He took a jar of beans and sprinkled them on the ground. Then, for a long time, he stared deeply into the beans.

"Hmmmmmmmmmmm," he said quietly.

"Hmmmmmmmmmm," echoed Willy.

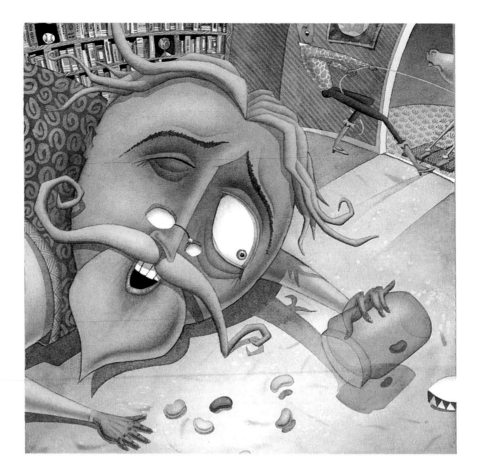

"Ohhhhhhhhhhhhh," he said sagely.

"Ohhhhhhhhhhhhh," echoed Willy.

"AhhhHHHHHHHHHH," he said loudly.

"AhhhHHHHHHHHHH," echoed Willy.

Finally the old man said, "Come closer, and I will tell you what kind of child you will have."

Willy moved closer.

The old man looked at him kindly and declared, "You will have either a girl or a boy."

Willy was elated, and he rushed home to tell his wife.

After a time the child was born, and it was indeed . . . a boy. Willy and his wife were overjoyed. "How wise the old man was," said Willy. "Now we must give our son a very special name."

But each time Willy thought of a name, it wasn't quite right. And each time his wife suggested a name, it wasn't quite right either.

"I know what I must do," said Willy one day. "I must go again to see the Wise Old Man. He will tell us the name of our child."

So once more Willy took a cow and went up the hills to the mountain of the Wise Old Man.

"Ah," the old man greeted him. "Have you come to partake further of my wisdom?"

"Yes," said Willy. "I need your help now more than ever."

"Well, come in, sit down, and tell me your troubles."

"My wife," said Willy, "had our child. And it was, just as you told us, a boy. We decided that for our son there must be a very special name. But we have thought and thought and cannot find the name. So I have come to you, hoping you will know the name of our child."

The old man nodded and said, "Yes, I think I can help you." Again he took a jar of beans, sprinkled them on the ground, and stared deeply into them.

"Hmmmmmmmmmm," he said quietly.

"Hmmmmmmmmmm," echoed Willy.

"Ohhhhhhhhhhhhh," he said sagely.

"Ohhhhhhhhhhhhh," echoed Willy

"AhhhHHHHHHHHHH," he said loudly.

"AhhhHHHHHHHHHH," echoed Willy.

At last the old man said, "Come closer, and hold out your hand."

Willy moved forward with his hand outstretched, and the old man whispered the name into his palm. Closing his hand quickly to protect the name, Willy called out his thanks and raced home to tell his wife.

He ran down the mountain and over the hills. Suddenly, in the fields on the edge of his village, he tripped on some stubble of corn. He fell . . . his hand came open . . . and the special name was gone!

Willy looked desperately at the ground. He could see nothing but corn stubble. Now how could he name his son?

He rushed to the village and gathered the strongest men to help him. Back in the field, they all dropped to their knees to search for the name, hoping they would know it when they saw it.

As they were looking, an old woman came along. She peered at the strange scene and called out, "What is happening here?"

Willy rushed over. "Oh, old woman," he cried, "this has been the worst day of my life." And he told her everything—how he had grown to be a young man, had fallen in love and married, had visited the Wise Old Man to learn the name of his son, and had fallen and lost the name.

"Oh my," said the old woman, "that is quite a story."

"Yes," said Willy. "And now I'll never know my son's name."

"Why," said the old woman, shaking her head, "it's simply ridiculous."

"It is?" exclaimed Willy.

And he rushed home to tell his wife that even though he had lost their son's name on the way home, the old woman had known it.

And so, Willy and his wife named their son . . . Simply Ridiculous.

Truly Foolish

Foolish behavior doesn't just happen in tales. Here are some funny anecdotes, inventions, records, and laws—and every one of them is true!

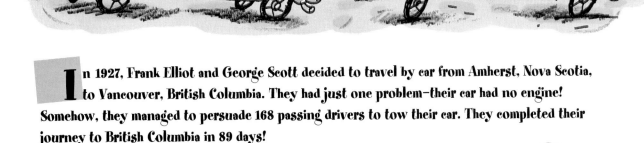

In 1927, Frank Elliot and George Scott decided to travel by car from Amherst, Nova Scotia, to Vancouver, British Columbia. They had just one problem—their car had no engine! Somehow, they managed to persuade 168 passing drivers to tow their car. They completed their journey to British Columbia in 89 days!

Ashrita Furman played 390 games of hopscotch in 24 hours, setting a record. Ashrita also holds the long-distance record for pogo-stick jumping—25.75 km in 6 hours and 40 minutes!

January 16 has been set aside as National Nothing Day. The organizers felt that it was important to have one day in the year when people don't have to honor, observe, or celebrate anything at all.

A woman won $12.3 million in a 1991 lottery, but she didn't claim her prize until seven weeks later. Why did she wait so long? She said it wasn't easy to get time off from her job!

PLEASE, BOSS, I NEED THE AFTERNOON OFF. I HAVE AN ITSY BITSY THING TO DO.

BOSS

Georges-Antoine Belcourt from Prince Edward Island was the first person in Canada to own a car. On his very first trip he proudly drove to the Sunday-school picnic, honked the horn to get everyone's attention—and then crashed into a fence post.

A gas-station attendant in Manitoba called police when a customer gave him a counterfeit $100 bill. How could he tell it was a fake? Instead of a picture of the Queen, the counterfeit bill had a picture of a chinchilla on it.

BEEP! BEEP!

A thief made a big mistake when he took his pager along to a robbery he committed. He left it behind by mistake, and it didn't take the police long to trace his identity from the numbers recorded on the pager.

It's illegal to pass another pedestrian on the right in Moose Jaw, Saskatchewan.

In 1900, Johann Hurlinger set a world record that still stands today. He walked from Vienna, Austria, to Paris, France, in 55 days—on his hands!

Bertha Dlugi invented the bird diaper for people who wanted to let their birds fly around the house. The tiny cloth diaper attached to a collar around the bird's neck.

The longest engagement on record was between Octavio Guillen and Adriana Martinez, of Mexico City. They were engaged for 67 years, and finally got married in June, 1969. Both the bride and groom were then 82 years of age.

A speech-writer who got bored invented a thumb-twiddling gadget. It had two holes, one for each thumb. The idea was to keep your thumbs apart for superior twiddling.

Gurning means making funny faces. Only one gurner in the world has won eight national titles at this peculiar sport— Ron Looney of Egremont, England.

Alfred A.D. Wolfrum of New Brighton, Minnesota, kissed 8001 people in 8 hours on September 15, 1990. That's one kiss every 3.6 seconds!

The world record for cherry-stone spitting was set by Horst Ortmann at Langenthal, Germany His cherry pit flew 26.76 metres.

It was risky to steal a geranium plant in early Upper Canada. You could go to jail for 5 years!

Don't try swimming on dry land in Santa Ana, California. There's a law against it.

In 1948, Alberta passed a law against Daylight Saving Time. You could be fined if you were found to be an hour ahead of everyone else.

It is against the law to pluck a duck in the market in Kingston, Ontario.

You may not take up more than one space on a park bench in Montreal, Quebec.

You can grow as tall as you like in Louisiana. The law says so!

IT WAS YOUR IDEA TO MOVE TO LOUISIANA. LOOK AT OUR DAUGHTER NOW!

It is against the law to jog recklessly in Fredericton, New Brunswick.

You may not borrow or lend water in Summerside, Prince Edward Island.

The Meadow

There once was a rabbit named Jason. He wanted to go to the meadow, but didn't know the way. So Jason went to the Wise Owl and said, "Wise Owl, which way is it to the meadow?"

"You go straight," he said as he pointed.

"Thanks, Wise Owl."

"But make sure not to go in the deep part of the meadow, for it is dangerous," warned the owl.

So Jason went off through the woods into the meadow.

"Wow! It's great here!" Jason saw the deep meadow and remembered the owl. Jason didn't care, and began playing in the forbidden zone. All of a sudden, a fox appeared out of his burrow.

"Help!" Jason cried as he ran from the fox.

Wise Owl swooped down and picked him up. "I told you never to go there!"

"I'll never do it again."

"Okay, but listen next time."

Leanne Zucchero
Grade 5

I like writing because it's a way to use your imagination and create your own stories. For me, I prefer to write about animals. I would like to continue writing when I get older.

Leanne Zucchero

The Mouse

A little mouse who had a cold,
(And had a touch of the flu I'm told),
Said with one loudly shaking sneeze,
"I must have just one bite of cheese."

So out of his hole he slyly did creep,
And ran past the pussy, fast asleep.
Crept into the pantry and on a gold tray,
Was the cake left from Grampa's hundredth birthday.

Chocolate, sticky, and topped with whipped cream,
(Seemed to the mouse he was in a good dream).
So onto the cake stepped his tiny wee claws,
And into the cake bit his tiny wee jaws.

And slurping and munching that dear little rat,
Ate till his tummy was so very fat,
That he had to sleep upon the lamp pole,
And he still can't fit into his little mouse hole.

Debbie Meyers
Grade 5

Little Kay

Written and illustrated by Robin Muller

ong ago there lived a magician and his three
daughters.

One day a message arrived from the Sultan
proclaiming that every noble household must send
a son to the palace to serve as knight for a year
and a day. This distressed the old magician greatly,
for he had no son, and he knew how ill-tempered and
unreasonable the Sultan could be.

His daughters sensed their father's unhappiness. "Papa,
why do you sigh so?" asked the youngest, whose name was
Little Kay. "Have we done something to displease you?"

"No, my dear," he answered. "No one could ask for sweeter
children. I am troubled," he said, "because the Sultan has
commanded me to send a son to be a knight at his court. If I
do not, I will surely be disgraced."

"Never fear," she said boldly. "Change me into a young man
with your magic and I will be our family's knight at court."

"Alas, I cannot," sighed her father. "You know my power
will not work beyond the boundaries of our land."

"Then I'll cut my hair short like a man's," cried Little Kay,
"and go to the Sultan's court in disguise!"

"A disguise is not enough," protested her father. "You must
be brave as well as clever—a true knight. For if the Sultan ever
found you out, he would feed you to the savage beasts he
keeps as pets."

"I am as brave as any knight," interrupted Morgana, the
magician's eldest daughter. "I insist on going. I would rather
risk my life than see you in disgrace."

At first the old man refused to consider such a wild

scheme, but at last he gave in to her pleas. With her hair cut short, dressed like a mighty warrior, Morgana set out full of confidence.

But the magician was deeply afraid of what might happen to his daughter at the Sultan's court, so he devised a plan to make her turn back. First he changed himself into a crow and flew ahead of her. Then, at the bridge that marked the border of his land, he transformed himself into an enormous lion.

When Morgana reached the bridge the lion sprang out with a terrifying roar, its red jaws fringed with dagger-sharp teeth. Morgana screamed and, forgetting her mission, raced for the safety of home.

Morgana tearfully told her father what had happened. "It's all for the best," he said. "I will accept my disgrace."

"No, you will not," declared Little Kay. "Let me—" But before she could finish, Tamara, the magician's second daughter, spoke up. "I will go as our family's knight," she said. "I am not afraid of a lion's roar."

The old magician tried every argument to dissuade her, but Tamara was adamant. With her hair cut short, armed with sword and shield, she rode out.

Once again the magician flew ahead, and this time changed himself into a ferocious boar. As Tamara approached, the boar rushed out, snorting and tearing the ground in front of her terrified horse. Screaming with fear, she turned her steed and raced back to her father's house.

"That's it!" cried the magician when he heard her tale. "There will be no more nonsense about pretending to be a knight."

"Oh, yes there will, Papa," piped up a fierce voice. Little Kay stood before him with her fists on her hips and her face scrunched into a most ferocious glare. "Now it's my turn!"

"My sweet pomegranate," he laughed, "even if the Sultan wanted to boil me in oil, I wouldn't dream of letting you try. You are far too young and small."

"Papa's right," said her sisters. "Where would we find armor small enough to fit you?"

"I shall make some," cried Little Kay. And she strode from the room.

Little Kay set to work with a hammer and tongs. Soon every room rang with the sound of her banging and clanging. She shaped an old platter and soup pot into armor, a teapot became a helmet, and from the fireplace she chose the largest poker for a lance.

Finally Little Kay went to the stable and took the old donkey that was deaf and nearly blind to be her steed. "Farewell," she shouted. "Look for me this time next year."

"Oh, dear," muttered the old magician sadly, "I'll have to

teach her a lesson too. One she'll never forget." And he whispered his spell.

As Little Kay drew near the bridge, the earth suddenly trembled. From a crack in the ground there came an ear-splitting roar and a wall of fire. Out of the flames rose a terrifying dragon, with bulging eyes and gaping jaws.

But Little Kay had prepared herself for a fearsome beast. Digging her heels into the donkey's flanks, she yelled, *"Charge!"* The little donkey, seeing and hearing nothing, galloped forward.

Little Kay dodged between the monster's huge legs, delivered a mighty whack to its rump and, with a leap and clatter, landed on the other side of the river.

Sore and worried, but secretly proud of his daughter, the old magician returned home.

When she arrived at the palace, Little Kay was escorted to the Sultan.

"Well," he sniffed, looking down his long and splendidly curved nose, "what have we here?"

"I am the magician's warrior son, Your Serenity," Little Kay answered proudly. "I have come to serve you for a year and a day."

The Sultan eyed the newcomer suspiciously. Not only was this knight clad in the oddest armor he had ever seen, but he seemed too small and too young to be of any use as a soldier.

"Is this the best the old magician can do?" he mocked. "He might as well have sent me a girl for all the use you'll be!"

He laughed at his own joke, then added with a cruel jeer,

"But no one would be stupid enough to send a girl to my court as a knight! Get along to the barracks. We'll soon find out how much of a warrior you are."

As the weeks passed the Sultan saw that Little Kay could indeed ride, joust, and swing a scimitar as well as any of the others. But he could not rid himself of the suspicion that all was not what it seemed. Deep in his heart he feared the old magician had tricked him by sending him a girl.

"What a ridiculous thought!" he said to himself. "Girls are not brave and clever as this little knight is. Nevertheless, I'll put him to the test. I will find out if I've been tricked!"

That night he told the cooks to put rings and brooches and necklaces in the porridge that would be served for breakfast the next morning. "If the little knight is a girl, this test will expose her as an imposter," he crowed. "Girls cannot resist pretty things. And woe to the magician if he has tricked me!"

In the barracks the next morning the usual breakfast chatter was broken by shouts of surprise and delight as knight after knight discovered some precious item in his bowl and held it up in wonder. "Look at this!" they said. "How beautiful!" "I love it!" "The Sultan must be pleased with us!" And they put on the jewels and gazed at one another in admiration.

All except Little Kay, who eyed the gifts suspiciously. "Why is the Sultan being so generous?" she wondered as she rubbed the porridge from a diamond clasp. "Here, you have it," she said to a server. "I have no use for such baubles." And she left to practise her archery.

The Sultan was annoyed that his scheme had failed and his suspicions grew darker. Every day the little knight seemed more skilled and more daring, but every day the Sultan grew more certain that he was being tricked.

"It's no use. I must try another test," he decided. "Perhaps some girls don't like jewellery, but no girl can resist draping herself in finery. I will fill the barracks with the most exquisite cloth, slippers, and plumes in the kingdom, and then we'll know the truth about the magician's child."

When the knights returned from their javelin lessons, they were amazed to see the barracks filled with bolts of shimmering silk, brocade of woven gold, satin shawls and feathers tinted with the hues of the rainbow.

"The Sultan must be displeased with the way we dress and this is his way of telling us," they cried. Without wasting a moment, they wrapped themselves in the fabulous cloth and twirled about, arranging and rearranging their gorgeous outfits.

All except Little Kay. "Fine feathers don't make a fierce falcon!" she scoffed. "If it's my clothes the Sultan

doesn't like, he can tell me to his face." And she left to get her lance sharpened.

Angry that another test had failed, the Sultan paced up and down in his sleeping chamber, scowling at himself in the mirror. Then suddenly his expression changed. "Of course! I know the answer!" he shouted. "The reason the jewels and gowns didn't work is that there were no mirrors to admire them in. No girl in the world can resist a looking glass."

When the knights arose the next morning they found the walls of the barracks brilliant with crystal mirrors. "How marvellous!" they cried, rushing to put on their finery so they could admire their splendid appearance. "We are the most beautiful knights in the world."

"This is really getting ridiculous," giggled Little Kay, gazing at her comrades' antics. "But I suppose boys will be boys." She left for her morning gallop.

With the failure of his latest test, the Sultan was beside himself with fury. "I am being tricked," he bellowed. "I know that I am being tricked. But how can I find out if that little villain is really a man or a maid?"

"That's very easy," said his housekeeper in surprise. "To tell if a person is a man or not, all you have to do is watch his throat when he drinks. If he's truly a man, his throat will bob like an apple. If it does not, she is most certainly a maid."

That evening the Sultan summoned all his knights to a great banquet. "Stand before me, magician's son," he said slyly to Little Kay. "I have been impressed by your swordsmanship."

Then he raised his goblet. "To the knights in my service, brave and true men, every one."

The knights raised their goblets to the toast and downed the wine. Every throat bobbed except Little Kay's. Hers remained as smooth as a marble column.

"Imposter!" the Sultan thundered. "Deceitful wretch! You and your vile family will suffer for this. Fetch me that scheming magician."

"Treacherous brood!" snorted the Sultan when the magician and his daughters were brought before him. "I have in mind a truly horrible punishment for your crime. Would you like to guess what it might be?"

But before anyone could utter a word, the palace shuddered as though hit by an earthquake. The great doors of the chamber burst open and there stood an ogre so huge and so hideous that the Sultan's brave knights fainted at the sight of him.

"I am Jabel," the ogre bellowed, "and today is my birthday! So what do you say?" he roared.

"Happy birthday, Jabel?" whispered the Sultan.

"And what do you do on birthdays?"

"Give presents?" added the Sultan weakly.

"Right!" howled the ogre with a wicked smile. "I have heard you give the most wonderful presents—jewellery and gowns and crystal mirrors. But you forgot to give anything to me!"

"What would you like?" whispered the Sultan.

"For a start I want all your treasure. If everything you have is not in a wagon at the gates in an hour, I will tear this palace down. And then I will squash ten thousand of your subjects like ants under my heel. Just for a start!"

"I am lost!" the Sultan wept when the ogre had gone. "Whatever I give him will never be enough. My kingdom will be destroyed. And not one of my knights is brave enough to stand up to him!"

"I am," piped up a fierce little voice. "I will defeat the ogre!"

"You?" cried the Sultan, gazing in wonder at Little Kay. "Impossible!" He waved at the unconscious knights on the floor. "I certainly can't give you an army."

"I don't need your army," replied Little Kay. "All I need is a small grey plum, a swallow from your battlements, and a leather sack to hold a special surprise. If I tricked someone as wise as you, Your Worriness, surely I can trick a stupid ogre!"

Hastily the Sultan agreed and within the hour a wagon piled high with treasure was at the palace gates.

"Happy birthday to me," roared Jabel. "What a wonderful start! I'll be back when I decide what I want for my next gift!"

As Jabel merrily rode the wagon through the forest, a little figure suddenly sprang out in front of him.

"Halt, ogre, and hand over that treasure—or I'll tear you apart!"

"What?" Jabel squinted down at Little Kay. "Why, you puny little runt! You would need fists of steel to pull me apart."

"That I have," Little Kay proclaimed. "My hands are so strong I can squeeze blood from a stone." Pretending to pick up a rock, she slipped the small grey plum into her hand and squeezed out a stream of sticky red juice.

The ogre stared in surprise, and then he began to snicker. "You can't fool me with that one. That's the old plum trick! Now get out of my way before I throw you over the mountain."

"You mean before I throw you," countered Little Kay. "My arm is so strong that I can fling a stone over the sun." She slipped the swallow into her hand, and with a mighty pitch, hurled the bird into the sky.

The ogre blinked as the dot disappeared into the sunlight, but then he grinned cruelly. "You can't fool me with that one either, you little slug. That was a bird. Out of my way before I skewer you."

But Little Kay stood her ground. She held up the leather sack. "Give me the treasure or my army will fill you with holes."

The ogre roared with laughter. "Now, that's a new one!" He snatched the leather sack.

"Be careful,' she warned. "They're asleep and they don't like to be wakened up."

Jabel held the bag to his ear. "I can hear them snoring all right," he sneered, "but I think I'll wake them anyway!" He gave the bag a might shake. "Let's see how they like that."

At once a black cloud of hornets swept out of the sack and furiously attacked him. Jabel howled with pain as they stung him again and again. "Brute!" he screamed as he tore through the forest. "Bully!"

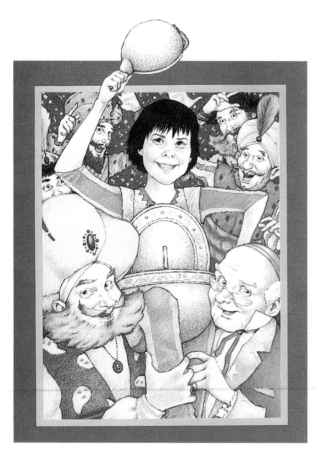

Little Kay shook her fist. "And don't come back!" she shouted at the disappearing ogre.

Little Kay marched triumphantly through the palace gates, the treasure in tow. Cheers rose from all sides as she passed, but when she reached the Sultan the crowd grew silent.

The Sultan smiled humbly. "Forgive me, Little Kay," he said. "I was wrong. You have proven yourself both brave and clever, and I appoint you Captain of my Royal Company of Knights." Again the crowd cheered.

"I have decided," he continued, glancing from Little Kay to her father, "that a proclamation shall be issued to every household in the kingdom. From this day forward, daughters as well as sons are welcome to serve at my court!"

The old magician smiled at the Sultan, and Little Kay grinned happily. Together they led the jubilant throng to the magnificent feast that awaited them.

ABOUT THE AUTHOR   ROBIN MULLER

As a teenager, Robin Muller found books so exciting while working in the warehouse of a children's book publisher that he decided to try his own hand at writing. He was very disappointed when publishers rejected his first book attempt, and it was ten years before he tried again. His second attempt was more successful, and he has now had many books published and won many awards, including the Governor General's Award for *The Magic Paintbrush*.

The Noblest Knight

by Eric A. Kimmel
Illustrated by Normand Cousineau

Eight hundred years ago, an English knight named Sir Hugh de Tabardie went to fight in the Crusades. Soon after arriving in the Holy Land, he fought his first battle. The Crusaders were defeated. Sir Hugh was thrown from his horse and captured.

The Muslim soldiers led their prisoners before the sultan, Salah-ad-din. Salah-ad-din talked with each one and set their ransoms according to their rank and fighting ability.

Ordinary soldiers had to pay a ransom of one hundred bezants. Squires had to pay a ransom of five hundred bezants. And knights like Sir Hugh had to pay a ransom of one thousand or more.

When Sir Hugh's turn came, Salah-ad-din said to him, "You have fought well. Your ransom is eight thousand gold bezants. We will hold you prisoner until it is paid."

"Noble Salah-ad-din," Sir Hugh replied. "I do not have eight thousand bezants. Were I to sell my horse, my castle, and all my lands, I could not hope to raise more than half that sum."

"Then you will remain a prisoner forever—unless you know another way."

"There is one," Sir Hugh answered boldly. "Allow me to return to the Crusader camp. I will ask my friends to help me. I promise to return in thirty days with the ransom."

"And if you fail to raise the money?"

"I will return nonetheless, and you may do with me as you wish."

The Muslim soldiers laughed long and hard at Sir Hugh's suggestion. What an idea—that Salah-ad-din would allow a captured knight to go free just by giving his word!

But Salah-ad-din did not laugh. "Very well, Sir Hugh," he said. "I will release you, if you will give me your word of honor that you will bring me your ransom in thirty days."

"I promise," Sir Hugh said.

Salah-ad-din continued, "However, if you return without the ransom, I will put you to death."

Sir Hugh did not flinch. "I will return in thirty days," he said, "even if it costs me my life."

Sir Hugh rode back to the Crusader camp. His companions were astonished to see him.

"How did you persuade Salah-ad-din to release you?" they asked him.

Sir Hugh explained. "He did not release me. He granted me thirty days to raise my ransom. After that time, I must return to his camp, whether I have the money or not."

"Then you are free," Sir Hugh's companions told him. "Salah-ad-din is our enemy. You do not have to keep your promise to him."

Sir Hugh hung his head. "My friends, you shame me with such talk. I gave Salah-ad-din my word. My word is my honor, and I will keep it, even at the cost of my life."

Some of Sir Hugh's friends contributed money for his ransom, but most refused. It made no sense for a man who was already free to pay a ransom. Besides, they agreed, promises with the enemy did not have to be kept.

Thirty days passed. At the end of that time, Sir Hugh de Tarbardie had raised only four hundred bezants. With sadness, he mounted his horse and rode back to the Muslim camp. Salah-ad-din's soldiers were astonished to see him, for they never expected a Crusader knight to honor a promise made to an enemy. They took Sir Hugh to the sultan at once.

"Sir Hugh, I am pleased to see that you have kept your word. Have you brought the ransom?" Salah-ad-din asked.

"I have collected only four hundred bezants," Sir Hugh replied. "I could raise no more."

"And yet you returned, knowing you were going to your death?"

"I gave my word," Sir Hugh answered.

Salah-ad-din turned to his commanders. "Behold this noble knight! He honors a promise made to an enemy, even at the cost of his own life. Surely, it would dishonor us to reward such nobility by putting him to death. Let us show the Crusaders that we, too, understand the meaning of honor. Which of you will contribute to Sir Hugh's ransom?"

Salah-ad-din passed a brass bowl among his commanders. Each one dropped a handful of gold coins into it. The bowl returned to Salah-ad-din, filled to overflowing.

Salah-ad-din counted out the money. "There are ten thousand bezants here. I will double it." He turned to Sir Hugh. "Your ransom has been paid many times over. You are free. Take these twenty thousand bezants with you. They are a gift from Salah-ad-din."

"I cannot accept them," Sir Hugh replied.

"Why not?"

"Noble Sultan," Sir Hugh began, "how can I accept riches for myself when I know that others still linger in captivity? Take back these twenty thousand bezants. Accept the money as ransom for as many prisoners as you will allow, and let them go free."

Salah-ad-din embraced the knight. "Sir Hugh," he said, "you may keep the ransom money. When you leave, take the prisoners with you. They are all free. I, myself, will pay their ransoms."

Sir Hugh de Tabardie led the newly freed prisoners back to the Crusader camp. When he returned to England years later, the story followed him there. Even when he was an old man, people would still point at him and say, "There goes Sir Hugh de Tabardie, the noblest knight who ever lived."

And Sir Hugh would always reply, "Not so. The noblest knight who ever lived was once my enemy. He taught me the meaning of honor and generosity. And if I could not be Sir Hugh, I would gladly be Salah-ad-din, for he is the noblest knight of all."

ABOUT THE AUTHOR   ERIC A. KIMMEL

Eric A. Kimmel says, "I love old things: old books, old pictures, old tools, old songs, and especially old stories. My earliest memories are of my grandmother telling me stories she remembered from her own childhood in Europe. The best present I ever received was a volume of Grimm's Fairy Tales, which I loved so much that I literally read it to pieces. Somehow, I always knew that I was going to be a writer when I grew up, and that I would share the stories I loved so much with others."

In Flanders Fields

The Story of the Poem by John McCrae

by Linda Granfield
Illustrated by Janet Wilson

In Flanders Fields

In Flanders fields the poppies blow
Between the crosses, row on row,
That mark our place; and in the sky
The larks, still bravely singing, fly
Scarce heard amid the guns below.

We are the Dead. Short days ago
We lived, felt dawn, saw sunset glow,
Loved, and were loved, and now we lie
In Flanders fields.

Take up our quarrel with the foe:
To you from failing hands we throw
The torch; be yours to hold it high.
If ye break faith with those who die
We shall not sleep, though poppies grow
In Flanders fields.

by John McCrae

May 1915. In Flanders, the French and Belgian lands bordered by the North Sea, it was the time for fresh green shoots and white blossoms. But the First World War had raged for nearly a year and winter's gloom remained, etched upon the skies by blackened tree trunks, ruined church spires, and barbed wire.

For nearly two weeks John McCrae, a Canadian medical officer, had attended to the horrible injuries suffered by soldiers in the continuing Second Battle of Ypres. While shells exploded around them, McCrae and his staff cared for hundreds of wounded men each day. And others, companions they had shared a meal with just hours before, were buried a few steps from the dressing-station door. McCrae later wrote, "We really expected to die in our tracks. We never had our boots off, much less our clothes."

On the second dismal day of May, one death in particular touched John McCrae. A close friend, Lieutenant Alexis Helmer, was killed early that morning when an enemy shell exploded at his feet. John McCrae, doctor, could do nothing to save him but John McCrae, soldier and friend, recited prayers as Helmer's remains were lowered into the Flanders soil and the grave marked with a wooden cross.

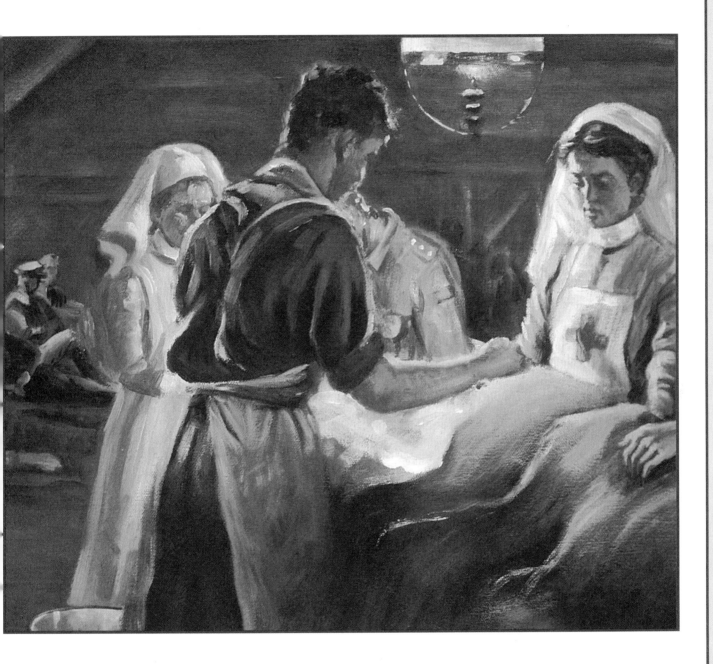

Reports concerning the hours after Helmer's burial differ. One states that McCrae sat on the back step of an ambulance, writing within sight of the new grave. Another says the doctor wrote off and on while bandaging the wounded. *What* he was writing, however, proved more important than *where* he wrote it. Helmer's death inspired McCrae to write "In Flanders Fields," a poem that to this day relays the images of war, loss, love, and renewal.

After he completed the poem, John McCrae was back at work in the dressing-station. The war was to continue for three more years . . . in Flanders fields and beyond.

Throughout history, the scarlet corn poppy has been a symbol of life. But after the publication of "In Flanders Fields" in 1915, it became a universal symbol of remembrance. The sturdy flower blossomed on the makeshift graves that were hastily dug during the war and, on the bombarded landscape of western Europe, seemed to thrive where nothing else could. Soldiers often picked the bright flowers and wore them on their helmets.

During the war, posters promoted wearing poppies in honor of the war dead. In 1919 a group of Americans, welcoming troops home, stripped the poppy decorations from a refreshment booth and left donations behind. Veterans' organizations soon realized that the demand for poppies could benefit disabled soldiers and families left in need by the war. The British and American Legions adopted the poppy as their memorial flower. By 1921 silk poppies made by French war orphans were among the first remembrance flowers sold in North America. Meanwhile, in Europe, the long process of reburying the war dead began. Soldiers' remains were moved from the battlefields to military cemeteries, and the crude wooden crosses were replaced by rows of neat stone markers

"Poppy mania" continued through the 1920s, and communities were urged to plant family and town poppy gardens. In Canada, John McCrae's homeland, there was even some talk of replacing the national symbol, the maple leaf, with a scarlet poppy.

Each year millions of poppies, reminders of the soldiers of the First World War and every conflict since then, are constructed of silk, plastic, paper, or felt. They are still handmade, and are sold by veterans and volunteers around the world. The funds collected are recycled into programs for veterans and their families.

 The scarlet blooms we wear on our labels today represent remembrance and life, just like the sturdy poppies that still blossom in the once-bloody fields of Flanders.

ABOUT THE AUTHOR   LINDA GRANFIELD

Linda Granfield, who grew up in Massachusetts, has lived in a suburb of Toronto, Ontario, with her family for the last twenty years. She has written eight non-fiction titles for children and their families, including the award-winning *Cowboy: A Kid's Album*. Linda likes to poke around museums, libraries, and dusty second-hand shops, looking for exciting bits of history to research for future books.

Remembrance Day

I think we should celebrate Remembrance Day to honor the soldiers and make sure they know we still remember them.

Also, we should thank them for giving their lives so we can live in peace.
But I also think we should have Remembrance Day for the people who came back from the war alive.

Eric Young
Grade 5

The Last Post

As the trumpet plays "The Last Post" at Remembrance Day ceremonies, I think of all those who went to war and all those who died. The moment of silence is solemn, and it makes you grateful that we have freedom in this land.

Shannon Carson
Age 12

I liked writing this because it reminded me of how lucky we are to be free.

Shannon Carson

Please Remember

I must ask you: do you know what Remembrance Day really is?
Do you think that it is only trying to remember some ordinary people fighting some big war?
Do you think that it is only remembering the blood?
No, it is not only these things...it is also remembering the good of the soldiers who went to fight for our country.
It is also remembering that they made the sacrifice of themselves so we could live today.
It is also remembering that if you lived in that time one of those people who gave their lives might have been your mother or father.
So please; I ask you to remember all those people who lost their lives in the war.

PLEASE REMEMBER

Jarrod Ursu
Grade 6